Spool Knit
Animals

This edition published in 2013
By SpiceBox™
12171 Horseshoe Way
Richmond, BC
Canada V7A 4V4

First published in 2012
English text, design and layout copyright © SpiceBox™ 2012
Original text and photographs copyright © Didier Carpentier 2011

ISBN 10: 1-77132-025-7
ISBN 13: 978-1-77132-025-2

CEO and Publisher: Ben Lotfi
Author: Cendrine Armani
Editorial: Trisha Pope
Creative Director: Garett Chan
Art Director: Christine Covert
Design & Layout: Charmaine Muzyka, Kirsten Reddecopp
Production: James Badger, Mell D'Clute
Sourcing: Janny Lam

For more SpiceBox products and information, visit our website:
www.spiceboxbooks.com

Manufactured in China

3 5 7 9 10 8 6 4 2

Contents

Introduction

Grab your spool knitting tool and a big ball of fluffy yarn, and curl up on the sofa—it's time to make some adorable animals! Spool knitting is the perfect craft to do on a rainy day, while you are watching your favorite TV show or are having a visit with your friends. It is a craft that allows your hands to be busy, but doesn't take a lot of your brain power—perfect!

Spool knitting (and it's close cousin—finger knitting) have been popular activities for centuries because it was how children learned the basics of knitting. Original spool knitting tools were simply an empty wooden thread spool with small nails hammered into the top, and they work just as well as the spool knitting tools used today! Once a length of knitted cord was produced, it was turned into anything from pot holders and place mats to hats and toys. We will show you how to make very cute critters, but you can experiment and come up with your own designs for your knitted cords. Once you start, you will become hooked on spool knitting!

Tools and Materials

Although spool knitting itself requires only the spool, a pick and the yarn, to make the animal projects in this book we recommend you gather a selection of craft supplies from around your home.

1 Assorted types and colors of yarn

2 Spool knitting machine or traditional spool

3 Scissors

4 Craft glue

5 Glue gun

6 Faux fur (black, yellow)

7 Pom-poms (various sizes and colors)

8 Styrofoam forms – balls, cones, eggs

9 Cotton balls

10 Large sewing needle

11 Wooden split balls

12 Acrylic paints

13 Paintbrush

14 Toothpicks

15 Pipe cleaners (various colors)

16 Felt and craft foam sheets (various thicknesses and colors)

17 Circles of craft foam (various colors)

18 Wooden hands and feet

19 Googly eyes

20 Nylon thread

21 Wood shapes – dragonfly, dolphin, butterfly

22 Key chain

23 Felt flowers (1 ½ in [4 cm] diameter, yellow)

9

8

21

18

16

6

2

10

14

17

3

15

DÉCO
ACRYLIC

DÉCO
ACRYLIC

12

11

7

19

22

MAT - MATT

Using the Traditional Spool

1 Thread the yarn down through the center hole of the spool, leaving a short tail hanging out the bottom, and the ball of yarn feeding from the top.

HINT: *You will find it much easier if you use a crochet hook to grab the yarn and pull it through the spool.*

2 Hold the spool knitter, wrapping the tail of yarn around your baby finger to keep it from slipping out. With your other hand, wrap the working yarn (the end attached to the ball) around the peg in front of you. Wrap it in a clockwise direction.

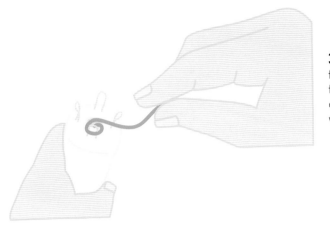

3 Still keeping the yarn tail wrapped around your baby finger, turn the spool clockwise, until the next peg is facing you. Wrap the yarn around this peg in a clockwise direction. Continue turning and wrapping until you have wrapped the yarn around all four pegs.

4 This is how your spool should look after you have wrapped all 4 pegs.

5 Hold the yarn in place with your index finger so it doesn't slip. However, don't hold the yarn too tightly, or you won't be able to make your stitch.

To make your first stitch, pass the yarn in front of the next peg, laying it above the yarn already wrapped around the peg from the previous step.

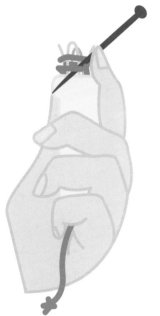

6 Use the wooden pick to scoop the bottom loop of yarn up and over the top yarn and over the peg.

7 Turn the spool and wrap the yarn in front of the next peg. Make a second stitch the same way you made the first: scoop the bottom loop of yarn up and over the top yarn and over the peg.

Continue turning the spool and making stitches. Every so often, gently tug the tail of yarn coming out of the bottom of the spool to tighten the stitches.

Finishing a Braid

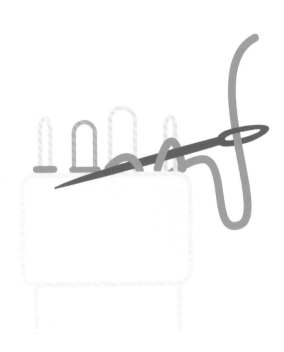

1 Unless the project instructions tell you otherwise, you should tie off your braid when you are finished, so it doesn't unravel. Cut the yarn about 6 inches (15 cm) beyond the end of your knitting. Thread the yarn through a darning needle, then with the loops still on their posts, pass the needle with the yarn through each loop.

2 You can now pull the loops off. Tighten the loops together by pulling on the yarn and sewing or tying a knot in the end.

Reinforcing a Braid

1 Take a piece of chenille pipe cleaner, fold it over ½ in (1 cm) from the end and carefully slide it into the braid.

2 Cut the pipe cleaner ½ in (1 cm) longer than the braid (see picture) so that you can stick it into the Styrofoam base if necessary.

3 If the braid is not going to be inserted into anything (see, for example, Adele on page 22) fold the pipe cleaner over and finish off the braid.

Covering a Styrofoam Base

1 Once you've finished off the braid, remove the braid from the spool knitter carefully and cut the yarn, leaving at least 6 inches (15 cm) length. Thread this onto a blunt sewing needle, and push the needle and yarn through the Styrofoam as you see in the photograph. Pull gently on the yarn until the braid stops it moving further. Cut the yarn ½ in (1 cm) from the end of the braid.

2 Put a few drops of craft glue on the Styrofoam base. Carefully wrap the braid round the base in a spiral.

3 When you've covered the base, cut the braid, leaving a 1 in (2.5 cm) length of yarn. Bring the 1 in (2.5 cm) of yarn into the center of the spiral and fix it in place.

Making a Cord

1 Cut eight strands of yarn about 1.5 yards/meters long. You can use one color or a mix. Knot the strands together at one end (A). Keep the strands in place by looping them round a doorknob or cupboard handle (B).

2 Using your fingers, twist the strands together, keeping them taut.

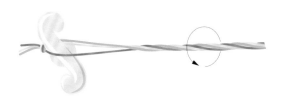

3 & 4 Fold the twisted yarn in half, holding the strands firmly with a finger just where the fold is. Unhook the strands from the doorknob or handle (B).

5 Remove your finger from the middle of the twist, without letting go of the loose ends. The yarns will twist up on themselves, making a cord. Finish off the cord by tightly knotting it and cutting off the excess yarn.

Spool Knitting Machine

This tool is a mechanized version of the traditional spool knitter on the previous page. It works more quickly and requires less effort. We think that the traditional tool allows you to enjoy the craft of knitting more, but if you are impatient to make your animal toys, then this is the way to go!

These knitting tools will come with instructions on how to set them up, so follow them closely for your machine.

TIP: *For the projects in this book, we use styrofoam shapes that correspond with the following sizes:*

	EGG	**BALL**
	IN/CM	IN/CM
Small:	(1 ¼ x 1 ¾ in / 3 x 4.5 cm)	(1 ¼ in / 3 cm dia)
Medium:	(1 ½ x 2 ¼ in / 4 x 5.5 cm)	(1 ½ in / 4 cm dia)
Large:	(1 ¾ x 2 ¼ in / 4.5 x 6 cm)	(2 in / 5 cm dia)

Projects

Lily the Mouse

2 ³/₄ in/7 cm long excluding tail

Materials:

- Gray yarn
- 1 medium Styrofoam egg
- Large sewing needle
- Felt (thin, gray, pink)
- Circle of craft foam
  (½ in [1 cm] diameter, pink)
- 2 googly eyes
- Pom-pom (small, pink)
- Nylon thread
- Craft glue
- Glue gun

ear template

1 Make a braid, 49 ½ in (125 cm) long, from the gray yarn. Wrap the braid round the egg, fixing it in place with craft glue.

2 Make a cord (see page 13) 4 ¾ in (12 cm) long for the tail and sew it to the back of the mouse.

3 Using the templates, cut out a large outside ear shape (A) from the gray felt and a small inside ear shape (B) from the pink felt. Glue the pink felt onto the gray with craft glue. Repeat to make a second ear.

4 Place the ears between two rows of braid on the mouse's head and fix them in place with the glue gun.

5 Use the glue gun to attach the eyes, the pom-pom (for a nose) and a little round foam circle for the mouth (see photo for size reference).

6 For the whiskers, cut six strands of nylon thread, each 6 in (15 cm) long. Use the sewing needle to thread the strands through the mouse's nose. Use a couple drops of craft glue to fix them in place and trim the ends.

Igor the Cat 3 ¼ in/8 cm high

Materials:

- Angora yarn (gray, white)
- 1 large Styrofoam ball
- Large sewing needle
- Felt (gray, pink, fuchsia)
- 2 googly eyes
- Nylon thread
- Pipe cleaner
  (15 ¾ in/40 cm, white)
- Craft glue
- Glue gun

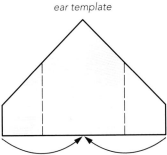

ear template

nose & mouth templates

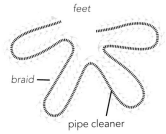

feet

braid —

pipe cleaner

1 Make a braid, 6 in (15 cm) long, from the white angora yarn.

2 Wrap the braid round the end of the ball, fixing it in place with craft glue, to make the nose.

3 Make a braid, 55 ¼ in (140 cm) long, from the gray angora yarn. Wrap this round the remainder of the ball, fixing it in place with craft glue. There should be some braid left hanging. Reinforce the excess braid with pipe cleaner to make the tail (see page 12). Finish off the braid (see page 11).

4 Make a braid, 9 ¾ in (25 cm) long, from the white angora yarn. Reinforce it with pipe cleaner to make the feet (see diagram). Sew the feet to the cat.

5 Using the template, cut out one outside ear from the gray felt and one inside ear from the pink felt. Glue the pink ear to the gray ear with craft glue. Gently fold in the sides (with the pink felt as the inside of the ear) and, using the glue gun, attach the ear to the cat's head between two rows of braid. Repeat with the second ear.

6 Use the glue gun to attach the eyes. Using the template, cut out a nose from the fuchsia felt and a mouth from the gray felt. Fix these in place with the glue gun.

7 See step 6 of Lily the Mouse, page 16, for how to make the whiskers.

Lola the Ladybug 4 ¼ in/11 cm high

Materials:

- Yarn (black, red)
- Large sewing needle
- Cotton ball
  (¾ in/2 cm diameter)
- Styrofoam half ball
  (1 ¼ in/3 cm diameter)
- Felt (red, black)
- 2 googly eyes
  (½ in/1 cm diameter)
- Pipe cleaner (black)
- 6 wooden beads
  (small, black)
- Craft glue
- Glue gun

mouth template

1 Make a braid, 11 ¾ in (30 cm) long, from the black yarn. Wrap the braid round the cotton ball, fixing it in place with craft glue, to make the head.

2 Make a braid, 15 ¾ in (40 cm) long, from the red yarn. Wrap it round the dome of the Styrofoam half ball in a spiral, fixing it in place with craft glue.

3 Make a braid, 8 ¾ in (22 cm) long, from the black yarn. Attach it in a spiral shape to the flat underside of the Styrofoam half ball, fixing it in place with craft glue.

4 Cut two pieces of pipe cleaner, each 1 ½ in (4 cm) long. Stick them into the head for the antennae. Stick a bead onto the end of each antenna and secure them with the glue gun. Bend the antennae into shape.

5 Cut two pieces of pipe cleaner, each 1 ¼ in (3 cm) long, for the arms, and two pieces, each 2 in (5 cm) long, for the legs. Stick them into the Styrofoam and secure them using the glue gun. Thread a bead onto the end of each piece of pipe cleaner and glue in place. Bend the arms and legs into shape.

6 Using the template, cut out a mouth from the red felt and attach it to the ladybug. Use the glue gun to attach the eyes.

7 Cut out four small circles from the black felt. Glue them to the ladybug's back.

8 Finally, sew a strand of black yarn down the center of the ladybug's back.

Arthur the Hedgehog 2 ¼ in/6 cm high

Materials:

- Yarn (beige)
- Angora yarn (brown)
- 1 medium Styrofoam egg
- Large sewing needle
- Felt (red)
- Two googly eyes
- Pipe cleaner (brown)
- Pom-pom (brown)
- Craft glue
- Glue gun

mouth template

1 Make a braid, 49 ¼ in (125 cm) long, with the beige yarn. Use the craft glue to attach it to the narrow end of the egg, wrapping it round to cover a quarter of the egg.

2 Make a braid, ½ in (1 m) long, with the brown yarn. Wrap it round the remainder of the egg, starting at the roundest part.

3 Cut two pieces of pipe cleaner, each 5 in (12.5 cm) long, to make the feet.

4 Bend the ends of the pipe cleaner pieces and use the glue gun to attach them to the underside of the hedgehog. (See photograph).

5 Using the template, cut out a mouth from the red felt and attach it to the hedgehog.

6 Finally, use the glue gun to attach the eyes and the pom-pom for a nose.

Inuk the Penguin 3 in/7.5 cm high

Materials:

- Yarn (black, white)
- Large sewing needle
- 1 medium Styrofoam egg
- Felt (thick, yellow)
- 2 googly eyes
- Craft glue
- Glue gun

1 Make a braid, 13 ¾ in (35 cm) long, from the white yarn. Wrap it round the front of the egg in a spiral, using craft glue to attach it. This will be the white of the penguin's tummy.

2 Make a braid, 35 ½ in (90 cm) long, from the black yarn, and use it to cover the rest of the egg.

3 Make three braids, each 1 ½ in (4 cm) long, from the black yarn. Fold them in two and sew the ends together to make two small wings and a tail. Sew them onto the penguin.

4 Using the template, cut out a beak and two feet from the yellow felt. Use the glue gun to attach these and the eyes to the penguin.

beak & foot templates

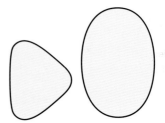

Materials:

- Yarn (black)
- 1 small Styrofoam ball
- Large sewing needle
- Felt (red)
- 2 googly eyes
- Pipe cleaner (black)
- Craft glue
- Glue gun

mouth template

1 Make a braid, 23 ¾ in (60 cm) long, with the black yarn.

2 Wind it round the ball, fixing it in place with craft glue.

3 Cut four pieces of pipe cleaner, all 4 ¾ in (12 cm) long. Shape them into feet and use the glue gun to attach them crosswise to the underside of the ball. (See diagram.)

4 In the center, use the glue gun to attach a small piece of pipe cleaner (A) to hold everything together.

5 Using the template, cut out a mouth from the red felt and attach it to the spider.

6 Finally, use the glue gun to attach the eyes.

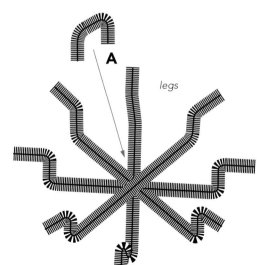

A

legs

Adele the Mouse
6 in/15 cm high (excluding feet)

Materials:

- Yarn (mauve, purple)
- Large sewing needle
- 1 large Styrofoam egg
- Styrofoam cone
  (2 ¾ in [7 cm] high)
- Felt (thick, purple)
- 2 googly eyes
- Pom-pom (small, black)
- Craft glue
- Glue gun

ear template

1 Make a braid, 55 ¼ in (140 cm) long, from the mauve yarn.

2 Wrap it round the egg, fixing it in place with the craft glue, to make the head.

3 Make two braids, each 39 ¼ in (1 m) long, one purple, one mauve.

4 Wrap them round the cone, fixing them in place with the craft glue, to make the body.

5 Using the purple yarn, make a braid 7 in (18 cm) long for the arms and a second braid, 7 ¾ in (20 cm) long, for the legs.

6 Sew the head, arms and legs to the body.

7 Using the template, cut out two ears from the purple felt. Set the ears between two rows of braid and use the glue gun to fix them in place.

8 Use the glue gun to attach the eyes and the black pom-pom for a nose.

Zoe the Caterpillar 8 ¾ in/22 cm long

Materials:

- Yarn (pink, fuschia, orange, green, turquoise, blue, black)
- Large sewing needle
- 5 small Styrofoam balls for the body
- 1 medium Styrofoam ball for the head
- Felt (red)
- 2 googly eyes
- 2 wooden beads (small, black)
- Pipe cleaner (black)
- Pipe cleaner (yellow)
- Craft glue
- Glue gun

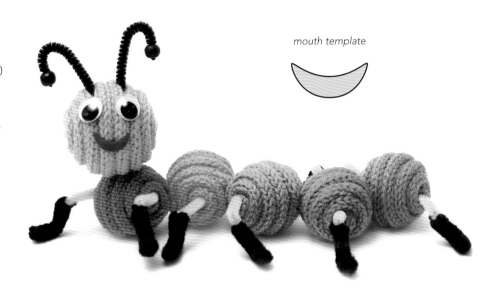

mouth template

1 Make five braids, one from each of the fuchsia, orange, green, turquoise and blue yarns, each 23 ¾ in (60 cm) long. Wrap each braid round a small ball, fixing them in place with the craft glue.

2 Make a braid, 39 ¼ in (1 m) long, from the pink yarn. Wrap it round the medium ball, fixing it in place with craft glue, to make the head.

3 Sew the six balls together to make a head with a body.

4 Cut two 2 ¾ in (7 cm) lengths of black pipe cleaner. Stick them into the head, between two rows of braid, to make antennae. Use the glue gun to attach a bead to the end of each antenna. Bend the antennae into shape.

5 Using the template, cut out a mouth from the red felt and attach it to the head. Use the glue gun to attach the eyes.

6 Make ten small braids, each one 1 ½ in (4 cm) long, from the black yarn to make the socks. Leave one end of each braid open.

7 Cut ten pieces of yellow pipe cleaner, each one 2 ¾ in (7 cm) long, to make the legs. Put a leg inside each sock then sew closed the socks around the pipe cleaner. (See Reinforcing a Braid, step 1–3 on page 12).

8 Stick two legs into each ball. Bend them to make the feet and knees.

Chloe & Lea the Ants 7 ¾ in/20 cm high

Materials:

- Yarn (burgundy, dark gray)
- Large sewing needle
- 1 small Styrofoam egg
- Cotton ball
  (¾ in/2 cm diameter)
- 1 small Styrofoam ball
- Felt (red)
- 2 googly eyes
- Pipe cleaner
  (red or black)
- Pair of wooden hands
- Pair of wooden feet
- Acrylic paint (red)
- Paintbrush
- Craft glue
- Glue gun

1 Make a braid, 23 ¾ in (60 cm) long, from the burgundy or dark gray yarn. Wrap it round the Styrofoam ball, fixing it in place with craft glue, to make the head.

2 With the same color yarn, make a braid 11 ¾ in (30 cm) long. Wrap it round the cotton ball, fixing it in place with craft glue, to make the thorax.

3 Make a third braid, using the same color yarn again, 20 ¾ in (60 cm) long. Wrap this one round the egg, fixing it in place with craft glue, to make the abdomen.

4 Cut 4 ¾ in (12 cm) of pipe cleaner (red or black) to make the arms. Sew the head, arms, thorax and abdomen together.

5 Cut two more pieces of the same color pipe cleaner, each 2 in (5 cm) long. Stick them into the top of the head, between two rows of braid, to make the antennae. Bend the antennae ¾ in (2 cm) from the end.

6 Cut two more pieces of the same color pipe cleaner, each about 3 in (7 cm) long, to make the legs, and stick them into the egg.

7 Cut two final pieces of the same color pipe cleaner, each 2 ⅓ in (6 cm) long, and fold them in half. Stick one end of each piece into the egg and stick the other end between two rows of braid on the thorax to make the middle pair of legs.

8 Using the template, cut out a mouth from the red felt. Using the glue gun, attach the mouth and eyes to the ant's face.

9 Paint the hands and feet red and leave to dry completely.

10 Apply a drop of glue from the glue gun to the ends of the arms and legs, then attach the hands and feet. Allow to dry.

Cleo & Sophie the Dragonflies 4 ¾ in/12 cm wide

Materials:

- Yarn (blue, white)
- Large sewing needle
- Two wood insect body shapes with pre-drilled holes for the wings (about 2 ½ in/6 cm long)
- 2 googly eyes
- Acrylic paint (blue, white)
- Paintbrush
- Glue gun

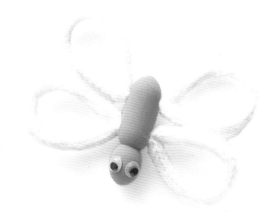

1 Begin by painting one wood shape blue and the other white. Let dry completely.

2 Make two braids, each 11 ¾ in (30 cm), from the white yarn. Thread them through the holes in the side of the blue dragonfly. Sew the ends of the braids to close them up.

3 Tuck the ends of the braids into the holes to make the wings.

4 Use the glue gun to attach the eyes.

5 Make two braids, each 11 ¾ in (30 cm), from the blue yarn. Use these to make the white dragonfly, following the same steps listed for the blue one.

6 Use the glue gun to attach the eyes.

Hal the Horse and Zack the Zebra 5 in/12.5 cm high

Materials:

- Yarn (brown for the horse, black + white for the zebra)
- 4 small Styrofoam eggs
- Large sewing needle
- Felt (black for the horse, black + pink for the zebra)
- Felt (thick, brown for the horse, black + pink for the zebra)
- 2 sets of googly eyes
- Pipe cleaner (brown for the horse, black for the zebra)
- Fun fur – brown for the horse's mane and tail, and black for the zebra's mane.
- Craft glue
- Glue gun

1 For the horse, use the brown yarn to make two braids, each one 23 ¾ in (60 cm) long. For the zebra, make two braids, each one 15 ¾ in (40 cm) long—one from the black yarn, one from the white.

2 For the horse, wrap each braid round an egg, fixing them in place with craft glue, to make the head and body. For the zebra, follow the same steps, but alternate the black and white yarn to make stripes.

3 To make the arms, make a brown braid for the horse and a black braid for the zebra, 6 in (15 cm) long. Reinforce the braid with 6 in (15 cm) of pipe cleaner (see page 12) and sew it to the narrowest part of the egg.

4 For the legs, make two brown braids for the horse and two black braids for the zebra, each one 3 in (7.5 cm) long. Reinforce the braids with pipe cleaner and sew them to either side of the animal's body.

ear template

(cut 4 in [10 cm] brown for the horse, 2 in [5 cm] black and 2 in [5 cm] pink for the zebra)

horse's mouth template

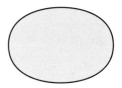

5 Sew the head to the body.

6 Using the template, cut out a mouth for the horse from the black felt and attach it to the head with craft glue.

7 Using the template, cut out four ear shapes from the brown felt for the horse. Cut two ear shapes in black felt and two in pink felt for the zebra. Bend them into shape and use craft glue to attach the inside of the ears to the outside (both inside and out are brown for the horse; use pink for the inside of the zebra's ears). Insert the ears between two rows of braid and use the glue gun to fix them in place.

8 Use craft glue to attach the fun fur to make a mane.

9 Use craft glue to attach a longer piece of fun fur to make the horse's tail.

10 Make a cord (see page 13) 2 ¾ in (7 cm) long from black yarn to make the zebra's tail. Sew it onto the back of its body.

11 Use the glue gun to attach the eyes to each animal.

Felix the Butterfly

3 ¼ in high, 3 ¼ in wide/8 cm high, 8.5 cm wide

Materials:

- Wooden butterfly shape
- Key chain
- Yarn (blue, turquoise, yellow, fuchsia, white)
- Large sewing needle
- Pipe cleaner (blue)
- 2 wooden beads (small, yellow)
- Acrylic paint (yellow)
- Paintbrush
- Glue gun

1 Begin by painting one side of the wooden butterfly. Let dry completely.

2 Slip a bead onto each end of the pipe cleaner and glue them in place to make the antennae. Bend them into shape and glue them to the wooden butterfly.

3 Make a braid, 2 ¾ in (7 cm) long, from the blue yarn and glue it lengthwise down the middle of the butterfly to make the body.

4 Make two braids, each one 6 ¾ in (17 cm) long, from the turquoise yarn and glue them round the outside edge of the butterfly.

5 Make two braids, each one 6 in (15 cm) long, from the yellow yarn. Then make two more braids, each one 2 ¼ in (6 cm) long, from the fuchsia yarn, and two braids, each one ¾ in (2 cm) long, from the white yarn.

6 Glue the braids to the butterfly, following the pattern in the photograph.

7 If you can't find a wooden butterfly shape, use the template to make your own.

template for wings

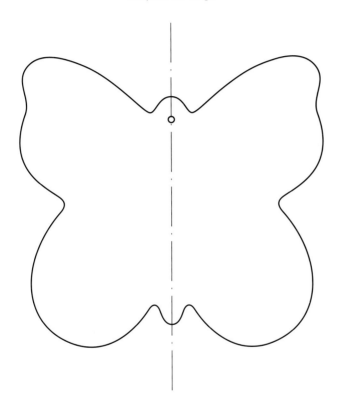

wooden butterfly shape

Materials:

- Yarn (dark gray)
- Large sewing needle
- 1 small Styrofoam egg
- Felt (thick, black)
- Felt (red)
- 2 googly eyes
- Pipe cleaner (black)
- Craft glue
- Glue gun

1 Make a braid, 31 ½ in (80 cm) long, from the dark gray yarn. Wrap it round the egg, fixing it in place with craft glue, to make the body.

2 Cut two pieces of pipe cleaner, each 2 ¾ in (7 cm) long, to make the arms, and two pieces, each 2 ⅓ in (6 cm) long, to make the legs.

3 Stick one end of each piece of pipe cleaner into the egg, inserting them between two rows of braid and using the glue gun to fix them in place. Bend the other end of each pipe cleaner ¼ in (1 cm) from the end.

4 Using the template, cut out a pair of wings from the black felt. Use the glue gun to attach the wings to the back of the bat.

5 Using the template, cut out a mouth from the red felt. Use the glue gun to attach the mouth and eyes to the bat's head.

6 Make a braid, 2 in (5 cm) long, from the dark gray yarn. Fold it in half to make an ear and sew it into shape. Make a second ear in the same way.

7 Sew the ears into place on the bat's head.

mouth template

template for wings

Sasha the Tortoise 3 ¾ in/9.5 cm long

Materials:

- Yarn (gray, green, yellow)
- Large sewing needle
- Cotton ball
  (¾ in [2 cm] diameter)
- Styrofoam half ball
  (1 ¼ in/3 cm diameter)
- Felt (red)
- Two googly eyes
- Pipe cleaner (gray)
- Craft glue
- Glue gun

mouth template

1 Make a braid, 11 ¾ in (30 cm) long, from the gray yarn. Wrap it round the cotton ball, fixing it in place with craft glue, to make the head.

2 Make a braid, 15 ¾ in (40 cm) long, from the green yarn. Use the craft glue to attach it in a spiral to the dome of the Styrofoam half ball to make the shell.

3 Make two braids, each 4 ¾ in (12 cm) long, from the gray yarn. Reinforce them with pipe cleaner (see page 12). Use craft glue to fix them in place on the flat side of the half ball to make the feet.

4 Make a braid, 2 in (5 cm) long, from the gray yarn to make the tail. Fix it in place with craft glue.

5 Make a braid, 8 ¾ in (22 cm) long, from the yellow yarn. Use the craft glue to attach it in a spiral to the flat part of the Styrofoam half ball to make the abdomen.

6 Using the template, cut out a mouth from the red felt and attach it to the tortoise's face.

7 Finally, use the glue gun to attach the eyes.

Paul the Dolphin 5 ¼ in/13.5 cm long

Materials:

- Wooden dolphin shape
- Yarn (blue, dark blue, white)
- Large sewing needle
- 1 googly eye
- Acrylic paint (blue)
- Paintbrush
- Glue gun

1 Begin by painting one side of the wooden dolphin. Let dry completely.

2 Make a braid, 17 ¾ in (45 cm) long, from the dark blue yarn. Glue it along the outside edges of the dolphin. (See photograph.)

3 Make two braids, one 11 ¾ in (30 cm) long and one ¾ in (2 cm), from the blue yarn.

4 Make a braid, 2 in (5 cm) long, from the white yarn.

5 Using the photograph as a guide, glue the braids to the dolphin. Glue the eye in place.

6 If you can't find a wooden dolphin shape, you can use the template provided to make your own.

template for dolphin

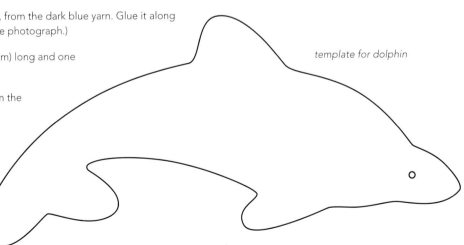

Edward the Pig 2 ¼ in/6 cm high

Materials:

- Yarn (pink)
- Large sewing needle
- 1 small Styrofoam ball
- Felt (thin, pink)
- 2 googly eyes
- 4 wooden beads (small, pink)
- 2 toothpicks
- Pipe cleaner (pink)
- Foam circle (pink)
- Craft glue
- Glue gun

1 Make a braid, 23 ¾ in (60 cm) long, from the pink yarn. Wrap it round the ball, fixing it in place with craft glue, to make the body.

2 Make a braid, 4 in (10 cm) long, to make a tail. Reinforce the braid with the pipe cleaner and finish it off (see page 12–13). Sew it onto the body and twist it into a corkscrew shape.

3 Cut the toothpicks in half. Stick them into the ball in preparation for making the legs. Using the glue gun, attach a bead to the end of each toothpick half. Let dry completely.

4 Using the template, cut out two ears from the pink felt. Place the ears on the head, between two rows of braid, and use the glue gun to fix them in place. Cut out the nose template from pink craft foam and use the glue gun to attach it to the face to make a snout. Finally, glue on the eyes.

ear template

nose template

Margo the Frog 4 ¼ in/11 cm high

Materials:

- Yarn (green)
- Large sewing needle
- Craft knife
- 1 small Styrofoam egg
- 2 Styrofoam half balls
  (1 ½ in/4 cm diameter)
- 2 wooden buttons
- Felt (red)
- 2 googly eyes
- Pipe cleaner (brown)
- Acrylic paint (green)
- Paintbrush
- Craft glue
- Glue gun

mouth template

1 Use the craft knife to cut ¼ in (5 mm) from the bottom of each Styrofoam half ball. Glue the trimmed half balls together with craft glue.

2 Make a braid, 23 ¾ in (60 cm) long, from the green yarn. Wrap it round the Styrofoam ball that you made, fixing it in place with craft glue, to make the head.

3 Make another braid, also 23 ¾ in (60 cm) long, from the green yarn. Wrap it round the egg, fixing it in place with craft glue, to make the body. Sew the head to the body.

4 Paint the two wooden buttons green and let them dry completely. Use the glue gun to attach an eye to the flat side of each button. Glue them to the frog's head.

5 Using the template, cut out a mouth shape from the red felt. Attach it to the frog's face.

6 Cut two pieces of brown pipe cleaner, each 2 ¾ in (7 cm) long, to make the arms. Stick them into the body at shoulder level, between two rows of braid. Bend the end of each pipe cleaner to make hands, then bend in the middle to make elbows.

thighs

feet

7 Make two braids, both 11 ¾ in (30 cm) long, from the green yarn. Reinforce them with pipe cleaner (see page 12). Bend them into feet/thighs, using the diagram as a guide. Sew them onto the body.

Bob and Sam the Bears 3 ¼ in/8.5 cm high (sitting)

Materials:

- Yarn (blue + dark blue or pink + fuchsia)
- Large sewing needle
- 2 cotton balls (1 in/2.5 cm diameter)
- 2 googly eyes
- 1 pom-pom (tiny, black)
- Pipe cleaner (7 ¾ in/20 cm, blue or pink)
- 2 wooden split balls
- Acrylic paint (blue or pink)
- Craft glue
- Glue gun

1 Make two braids, each 19 ¾ in (50 cm) long, one from the blue yarn and one from the dark blue yarn (or one fuchsia and one pink). Wrap each braid around a cotton ball, fixing them in place with craft glue, to make the head and body.

2 Make a braid, 4 ¾ in (12 cm) long, from either blue or pink yarn, and reinforce it with pipe cleaner (see page 12) to make the arms.

3 Sew the head and arms to the body.

4 Make two braids, each 1 ½ in (4 cm) long, from either blue or pink yarn. Reinforce the braids, bend them into shape to make legs and use the glue gun to attach them to the body.

5 Paint the two wooden split balls, either blue or pink. Let dry completely. Using the glue gun, attach them to the head to make the ears.

6 Use the glue gun to attach the black pom-pom for the nose and the eyes.

Jules the Chick 3 ¼ in/8 cm high

Materials:

- Yarn (yellow)
- Large sewing needle
- 1 large Styrofoam egg
- Felt (thin, yellow)
- Felt (thick, orange)
- 2 felt flowers
  (1 ½ in/4 cm diameter, yellow)
- 2 googly eyes
- Fun fur (yellow)
- Craft glue
- Glue gun

1 Make a braid, 47 ¼ in (120 cm), from the yellow yarn. Wrap it round the Styrofoam egg, fixing it in place with craft glue. Have the narrow part of the egg facing up.

2 Using the template, cut out a beak from the orange felt. Use the glue gun to fix it in place.

3 Use the glue gun to attach the eyes to the face and the fun fur to the top of the chick's head.

4 Using the template, cut out two wings from the yellow felt. Use the glue gun to attach one to each side of the chick's body.

5 Use the glue gun to attach the felt flowers* to the bottom of the egg to make the feet.

You can use the photograph as a guide for making your own flowers.

templates for beak and wing

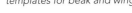
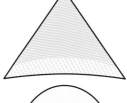

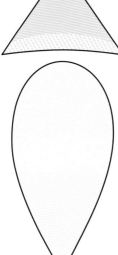

felt flower (foot) - actual size

Templates

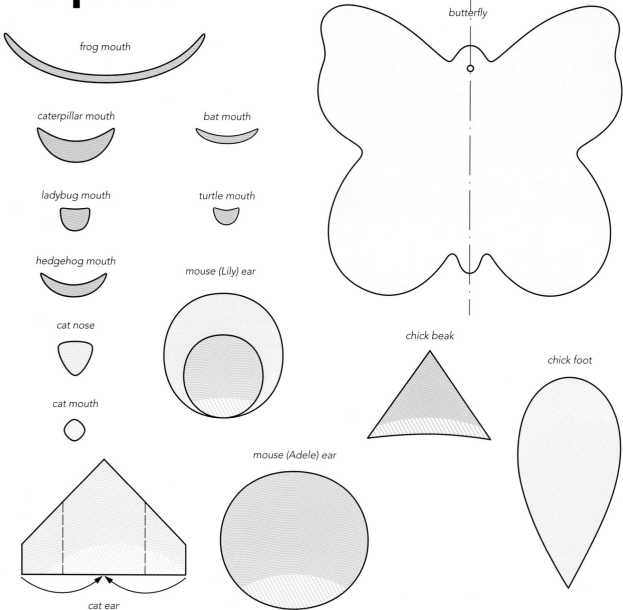

frog mouth

caterpillar mouth

bat mouth

butterfly

ladybug mouth

turtle mouth

hedgehog mouth

mouse (Lily) ear

cat nose

chick beak

chick foot

cat mouth

mouse (Adele) ear

cat ear

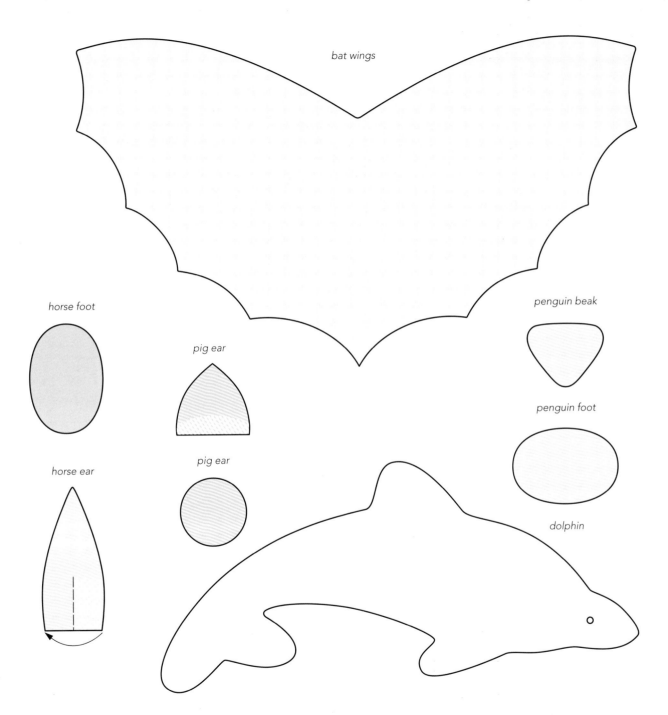

bat wings

horse foot

pig ear

penguin beak

pig ear

penguin foot

horse ear

dolphin